✱ STYLE IT: TRENDS AND FADS

Hat Hype

by VIRGINIA LOH-HAGAN

45th Parallel Press

Published in the United States of America by
Cherry Lake Publishing Group
Ann Arbor, Michigan
www.cherrylakepublishing.com

Reading Adviser: Beth Walker Gambro, MS, Ed., Reading Consultant, Yorkville, IL
Book Designer: Joseph Hatch

Photo Credits: Wavy_ revolution/Pexels.com, cover; RDNE Stock project/Pexels.com, 4; Artem Podrez/Pexels.com, 7; Louvre Museum via Wikimedia Commons, 8; Maria Mariscal via Wikimedia Commons, 11; Pierre Charles Comte, Public domain, via Wikimedia Commons, 13; Image courtesy of Lee Kim, 14; Kingsley studio, Public domain, via Wikimedia Commons, 16; © Cavan-Images/Shutterstock, 19; Lance Reis/Pexels.com, 21; khamla douangchandeng/Pexels.com, 22; cottonbro studio/Pexels.com, 24; cottonbro studio/Pexels.com, 27; Ksenia Chernaya/Pexels.com, 28; Public Doman, Prints and Photographs Division, Library of Congress, 31

Copyright © 2026 by Cherry Lake Publishing Group

All rights reserved. No part of this book may be reproduced or utilized in any form or by any means without written permission from the publisher.

45th Parallel Press is an imprint of Cherry Lake Publishing Group.

Library of Congress Cataloging-in-Publication Data has been filed and is available at catalog.loc.gov

Cherry Lake Publishing Group would like to acknowledge the work of the Partnership for 21st Century Learning, a Network of Battelle for Kids. Please visit Battelle for Kids online for more information.

Note from publisher: Websites change regularly, and their future contents are outside of our control. Supervise children when conducting any recommended online searches for extended learning opportunities.

Printed in the United States of America

Dr. Virginia Loh-Hagan is an author and educator. She is currently the Executive Director for Asian American Native Hawaiian Pacific Islander Affairs at San Diego State University and the Co-Executive Director of The Asian American Education Project. She lives in San Diego with her very tall husband and very naughty dogs.

TABLE of CONTENTS

INTRODUCTION **5**
CHAPTER 1: **Perfume Cones** **9**
CHAPTER 2: **Veiled Hats** **10**
CHAPTER 3: **Hennins**................................**12**
CHAPTER 4: **Picture Hats** **15**
CHAPTER 5: **Top Hats** **17**
CHAPTER 6: **Panama Hats** **18**
CHAPTER 7: **Newsboy Caps** **20**
CHAPTER 8: **Baseball Caps** **23**
CHAPTER 9: **Beanies**................................ **25**
CHAPTER 10: **Bucket Hats** **26**

DO YOUR PART! **29**
GLOSSARY **32**
LEARN MORE **32**
INDEX... **32**

There are always new hat trends! Which ones have you seen lately?

INTRODUCTION

Everybody has style. Some people have more style than others. They stand out. They use **fashion** to express themselves. Fashion is about how people want to look. It's about how people dress. It includes clothes, shoes, hats, and jewelry. It also includes hairstyles and makeup.

Fashion changes across cultures. It changes over time. There are many fashion **trends**. Trends are fads. They're patterns of change. They reflect what's popular at a certain time. Many people copy popular looks. They copy famous people. They get inspired. They want to be cool. They want to be in style.

Some trends last a long time. Other trends are short. All trends make history.

Hats are head coverings. Most have a **crown**. Crowns fit over the head. Some hats have a **brim**. Brims extend outward. Most hats stay on heads. Some need **hatpins**. Hatpins secure hats to heads.

Hats are worn for different reasons. They protect a person's head. They keep the head warm. They're part of special traditions. They're required for some jobs. They're also worn for fashion.

Hats can change how people look. They add beauty. They add personality. They add style. They signal one's role in society. They play a key role in fashion.

Some hats are big. Some are small. Some are fancy. Some are simple. There have been a lot of hat trends. This book features some of the fun ones!

Hats can add a lot to someone's personal style.

Ancient Egyptians would wear cone hats over wigs or shaved heads.

Perfume Cones

Ancient Egyptians were very clean. They bathed several times a day. They even wore special hats. These hats hid body odors. These hats were shaped like cones. They were made of wax. The wax was made from oils, fat, and **resin**. Resin is a thick, sticky substance produced by some trees and plants in response to injury. It smells good. It's used to make perfumes.

People wore these cone hats. They also wore headbands. Their body heat warmed the cones. The cones would slowly melt. This released good scents. Wax would drip onto clothes. This formed stripes.

These hats may have also been used to **purify**. Purify means to clean. Ancient Egyptians cared about life after death. They wanted to purify their spirits.

CHAPTER

TWO

Veiled Hats

The **weimao** is a Chinese veil hat. It's also known as a curtained hat. It was popular around 600 to 900 BCE. It had a wide brim. A veil hung around the brim. It draped down to the shoulders. Some veils had designs.

The veils protected women from the Sun. They protected women from wind. They also protected women's bodies from being seen.

Laws forced women to wear longer veils. Mili hats covered the whole body. Trends changed. Rich noblewomen wore weimao hats instead. These hats only hid their faces. Women wore them when they left the house. Men could also wear them.

FASHION-FORWARD PIONEER

Gilbert Marquez is Mexican American. He traveled between the United States and Mexico. He sold tequila. He met someone who made sombrero hats. Sombreros are Mexican straw hats. They have wide brims. They have high, pointed crowns. They shield workers from the sun. Marquez was inspired to make hats. In 2017, he started Pachuco Supply Co. He bought old hats. Someone was throwing them away in Mexico. Marquez said, "I knew that recycling, repurposing, and upcycling was important. And there's something about an old hat that just has so much soul." He watched YouTube videos. He learned to make hats. He wanted to honor the Pachuco culture. Pachucos were Mexican American youths. They were known for their flashy clothes.

Pachuco style includes big suits, chains, and stylish hats.

CHAPTER

THREE

Hennins

Hennins were tall headdresses. They were shaped like cones. Some had flat tops. Some had pointed tops. Hennins were made of light material. They had long veils attached to the top. The veils could be several feet long.

They were trendy in the 1400s. They were worn by European women. They were worn by rich women. The taller the hennin, the higher the rank.

Women wore hennins tilted backward at an angle. This showed off their foreheads. They would also pluck or shave their foreheads. They did this to raise their hairlines. They tied their hair back. Some hid their hair under the hennins. Some left their hair loose behind the hennins.

Today, we know hennins from pop culture. Fairytale princesses are often shown wearing hennins.

FASHION REBEL: TRENDSETTER

Lee Kim is promoting wearable art. In 2017, she forgot her friend Tracy Brandenburg's birthday. Kim felt bad. She bought pipe cleaners. She made a birthday hat. She sent a picture to Brandenburg. This sparked an idea. Kim made more pipe cleaner hats. She called them "Wearable Tracy" hats. She walked around in them. People noticed her. They smiled. It helped her feel seen. It made her more social. She created her own challenge on Instagram. She had 3 rules:

(1) Make a new hat every morning.
(2) Wear it all day long.
(3) Talk to people who ask about her hat. Kim said this project made her feel bold.

CHAPTER  four

Picture Hats

Picture hats are large. They're elegant. They have very wide brims. The brims framed the face. This created a round picture frame effect. These hats were trendy in the late 1700s.

They were made popular by Thomas Gainsborough. Gainsborough was an English painter. He painted many royals. He often painted royal women with big hats. These hats are also known as Gainsborough hats.

These hats were great for **trimmings**. Trimmings are decorations. They add color. They add more fun. Women added feathers. They added ribbons. Some even added stuffed birds.

Big hats went out of style with World War I (1914–1918). People became more reserved. But big hats have made several comebacks.

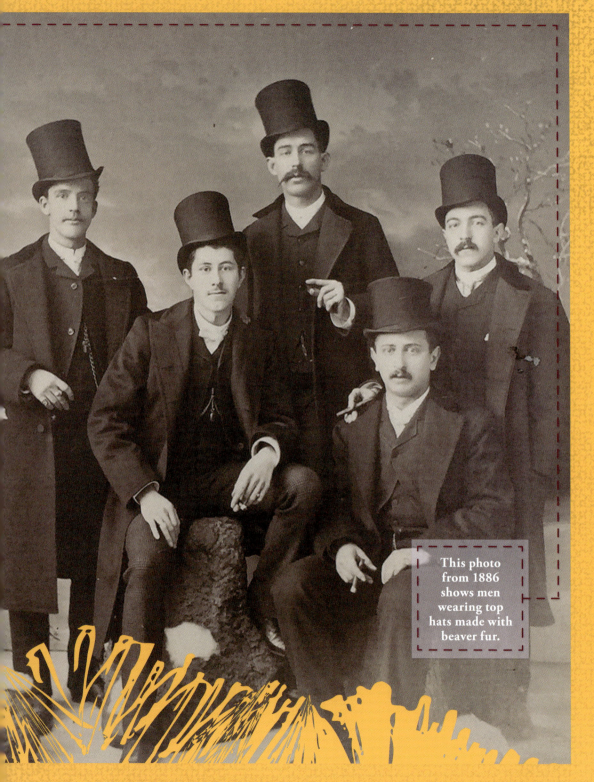

This photo from 1886 shows men wearing top hats made with beaver fur.

CHAPTER

five

Top Hats

Top hats are tall. They're named for looking "top-heavy." They're also called high hats or toppers. They're like tubes. They have flat tops. They have small brims.

Most top hats were 8 inches (20.3 centimeters) high. Some were 12 inches (30.5 cm) high. Early top hats were made from felt. This felt was made from fur. Later versions used shiny silk fabric. This fabric was glued onto cardboard. This gave a smooth finish.

Top hats were popular in the 1700s to early 1900s. They were a sign of class. Men in the middle and high classes wore them. They wore them for formal events. They wore them with suits. Today, top hats are still part of formal wear.

Panama Hats

Panama hats are not from Panama. They're from Ecuador. They were shipped through Panama. That's how they got the name.

They've been worn for more than 500 years. But they became trendy in the 1800s. In 1906, President Theodore Roosevelt visited the Panama Canal. He wore a Panama hat. This made the name even more popular.

Panama hats have wide brims. They're made from straw. They have a tight weave. They have a black hatband. They're light. They keep people cool. They are popular summer hats. They go with everything. They were a classic hat style for men in the early 1900s. They have gone in and out of fashion since then.

DIY FASHION FUN

You can even try adding flowers to hats!

PEOPLE WEAR MANY HATS. MAKE YOUR OWN HATS. HERE ARE SOME IDEAS:

» Add your own designs to hats. There are several ways to do this. Sew and stitch on designs. Use heat to transfer designs. Paint on designs. Iron on patches.

» Add sparkle to hats. Make your hats more fun. Add tassels. Add pom-pom balls. Add ribbons. Add a necklace around the crown. This can look like a hatband. Hatbands go around the crown.

» Cut out triangles in the hat brim. This lets light through. It makes patterns of light over hair and clothes.

Newsboy Caps

Newsboy caps have soft crowns. They're flat. They have **visors**. Visors are curved and stiff. They stick out in front of hats. They give shade. They protect the eyes.

The caps were trendy in the late 1800s and early 1900s. Boys sold newspapers. They wore these caps. That's how the caps got their name. But other working-class men wore them, too. They were worn in Europe and North America.

Rich men also wore these caps. They wore them for **leisure** activities. Leisure is free time. Newsboy caps were a great substitute for top hats. They could be worn all the time. They were also called golf hats or driving hats.

Today, women also wear newsboy caps.

CHAPTER

EIGHT

Baseball Caps

The first official baseball team was from New York. They were the New York Knickerbockers. The players wore the first baseball caps. They did this in 1849. They were made of straw. The caps kept the sun out of their eyes. This helped them play better. Baseball cap designs evolved and improved.

Baseball caps are soft. They have rounded crowns. They have stiff visors or bills. They have **logos** in the front. Logos are like team signs.

In the 1980s, baseball caps became a fashion trend. Sports TV was popular. Fans wore baseball caps to support their teams. Hip-hop was also popular at this time. Many rappers wore baseball caps. Baseball caps are still popular.

Today, baseball caps go beyond baseball.

Today, people wear teeny beanies. These beanies are worn high across the forehead.

CHAPTER

nine

Beanies

Beanies are soft knitted hats. They don't have brims. They hug the head. They're mostly made of yarn.

Beanie is thought to come from *bean*. *Bean* was an American slang word for "head." Workers and sailors have been wearing them since the 1400s. Beanies keep the head warm and dry. They keep hair out of people's faces.

In the 1950s, many college students wore beanies. The hats really took off in the 1990s. Skaters and hip-hop artists wore beanies. Beanies gave a cool, edgy vibe. They have been a huge fashion trend ever since.

CHAPTER

Bucket Hats

Bucket hats are made from heavy fabrics. They're soft. They have narrow brims. Their brims slope down. They stop water from dripping onto the face. They fit tightly.

They first emerged around 1900. They were worn by Irish farmers and fishermen. They're comfortable. They're easy to pack. They can be folded. They can even fit in pockets.

They're more than just outdoor clothes. They can be dressed up or down. They became fashionable in the 1960s. Hippies and surfers wore them. But hip-hop rappers made them hot. They wore them in the 1980s. Today, bucket hats keep trending.

Today, bucket hats are more on trend than ever.

There are plenty of hats made from plant materials.
Look for one the next time you shop!

DO YOUR PART!

It's always fashionable to stand up for what's right. Fashion can be more than just about looks. It can be used to fight for causes. Be a fashion **activist**. Activists fight for change. They want a better world. Here are some ways to make a difference:

- Wear **cruelty-free**, **vegan** clothes. Cruelty-free means no animals were harmed. Vegan means no animals were used. Avoid leather. Avoid wool. Avoid silk. Avoid fur and feathers. Instead, buy clothes made from plants. These materials include cotton, linen, and bamboo. Protect animals while still wearing great clothes.

- Wear hats made of recycled **fibers**. Fibers are like plant hair. They're made into fabrics. Old clothes or old hats are taken apart. Their fibers are reused. New hats are made. This protects the planet. It reduces waste. It doesn't add to **landfills**. Landfills are spaces that bury waste.

- Buy local. Buy high-quality hats. They may cost more. But you don't need a lot of hats. You just need a few good hats. Hats can be worn many times. Avoid cheap, **mass-produced** hats. This means making large numbers of goods. They're often made with large machines in factories.

Remember, every little bit counts. Kindness matters. You can look good and feel great!

FIGHTING FOR JUSTICE

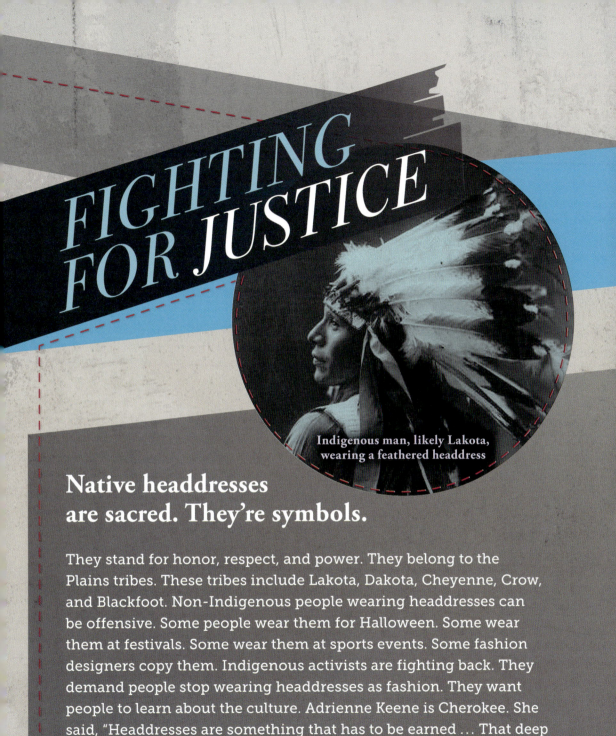

Indigenous man, likely Lakota, wearing a feathered headdress

Native headdresses are sacred. They're symbols.

They stand for honor, respect, and power. They belong to the Plains tribes. These tribes include Lakota, Dakota, Cheyenne, Crow, and Blackfoot. Non-Indigenous people wearing headdresses can be offensive. Some people wear them for Halloween. Some wear them at festivals. Some wear them at sports events. Some fashion designers copy them. Indigenous activists are fighting back. They demand people stop wearing headdresses as fashion. They want people to learn about the culture. Adrienne Keene is Cherokee. She said, "Headdresses are something that has to be earned … That deep sacred meaning is eclipsed by the desire to just dress up and play Indian."

Glossary

activist (AK-tih-vist) person who fights for political or social change

brim (BRIM) part of the hat that extends outward from the base of the crown and around the sides of the head

crown (KROWN) main part of the hat that covers the head

cruelty-free (KROOL-tee-FREE) free from animal testing

fashion (FAA-shuhn) any way of dressing that is favored or popular at any one time or place

fibers (FIE-berz) thin pieces of plant material used to make fabric

hatpin (HAT-pihn) long pin that holds a hat in position by securing it to hair

hennins (HEH-nuhnz) tall headdresses shaped like cones

landfills (LAND-filz) places to bury trash and waste material

leisure (LEE-zhuhr) free time

logos (LOH-gohz) symbols or designs adopted by an organization to identify its products or brand

mass-produced (maas-pruh-DOOST) making large numbers of goods, often by machines in factories

purify (PYUR-uh-fiye) to clear of harmful materials

resin (REH-zuhn) scented, sticky substance produced by some trees and plants in response to injury

trends (TRENDZ) fads or changes that are popular or common

trimmings (TRIH-mingz) decorations

vegan (VEE-guhn) containing no animal products

visors (VIE-zerz) pieces on the front of hats that shade the eyes

weimao (WAY-mow) a Chinese veil hat

Learn More

Croll, Jennifer. *Bad Boys of Fashion: Style Rebels and Renegades Through the Ages.* Toronto, ON: Annick Press, 2019.

Loh-Hagan, Virginia. *Far-Out Fashion.* Ann Arbor, MI: Cherry Lake, 2018.

Loh-Hagan, Virginia. *Fashion.* Ann Arbor, MI: Cherry Lake, 2021.

Millar, Christine Na-Eun. *History Is Worn: A Story of Fashion.* Los Angeles, CA: Honest History, 2023.

Index

Ancient Egyptians, 8–9
animal materials, 16–17, 29, 31
artworks, 14

baseball caps, 7, 22–23
beanies, 24–25
bucket hats, 26–27

caps, 7, 20–23
cone hats, 8–9, 12–13
creating and crafting, 11, 14, 19
cruelty-free clothing, 28–29
cultural details, 9–11, 18, 31
curtained hats, 10

ethical clothing, 28–30

fashion, 5
fashion designers, 11, 31
formality and status of hats, 10, 12, 15–17, 20
functionality of hats, 6, 9–11, 15, 18, 23, 25–26

Gainsborough, Thomas, 15

hairstyles, 5, 12
hats, 6
headdresses, 12–13, 31
hennins, 12–13

Kim, Lee, 14

logos, 23

Marquez, Gilbert, 11

Native headdresses, 31
newsboy caps, 20–21

Pachuco style, 11
Panama hats, 18
perfume cones, 8–9
personal style, 5, 6–7, 11, 14, 20, 23, 25
picture hats, 15

Roosevelt, Theodore, 18

sombreros, 11
sports team caps, 23
structures of hats, 6, 9–12, 14, 16–18, 20, 23, 25–26
sustainability, 11, 28–30

traditional headdress, 31
trends, 4–5, 8–13, 15–18, 20–27
trimmings, 15, 19

upcycling, 11, 19, 30

vegan clothing, 28–29
veiled hats, 10, 12–13
visors, 20–21, 23

wearable art, 14
weimao hats, 10